VEGETARIAN RECIPES FROM
THE AFRICA MISSION FIELD

'TIL WE EAT AGAIN

Compiled and written by Kristina Trajkov
Photography by Kristina Trajkov
Layout and design by Erin Engle
Art Director: Sam Godfrey

Published by Amazing Facts
P.O. Box 1058
Roseville, CA 95678
(916) 434-3880
Order Dept: (800) 538-7275
afbookstore.com

THANK YOU

We thank you on behalf of the children and their families who, because of this cookbook, are now able to afford treatments for common illnesses in one of the poorest districts in Malawi, Africa.

malamulohospital.org

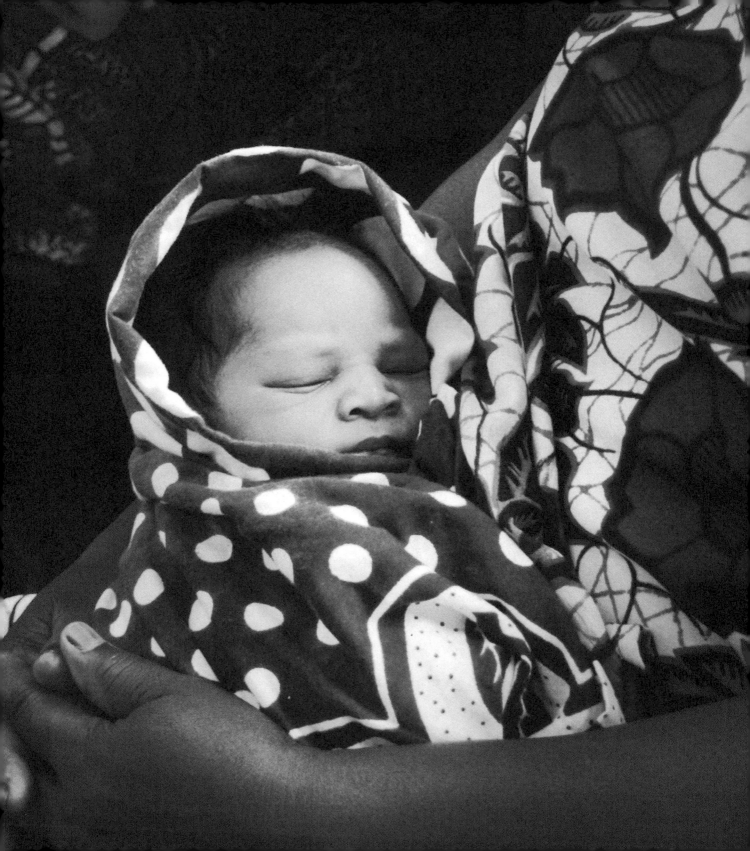

FOREWORD

'Til We Eat Again aims to depict the everyday lifestyle of a volunteer at Malamulo Hospital, gathering together meal after meal with amazing dishes served up every time. When first arriving at Malamulo, many of us experienced the trauma of not knowing what or how to cook on a daily basis. We no longer had access to the luxuries we were familiar with in our home countries.

At the same time, we saw a huge need for local families and their children under the age of five to have inexpensive access to medications and treatment for common illnesses, such as malaria and gastroenteritis. What better way to raise some funds to help these poor families and address the cooking confusion of volunteers that visit Malamulo, all at the same time? This is how this book was developed and how it came to be in your hands.

All of the recipes are vegetarian, and all of the ingredients are accessible locally. Some are well-known culinary classics, while others are not so well known and might even surprise you! They have been gathered from various individuals who are either current or former volunteers at Malamulo.

We would like to acknowledge and thank every single person that contributed toward this cookbook—whether it was through providing the recipes, preparing the dishes for the photographs, or assisting with eating the dishes! We could not have completed this cookbook without you.

We sincerely hope that you enjoy this cookbook and find it useful, and that it will help you attain new culinary heights. But most of all, we thank you on behalf of all the children and their families who, because of this cookbook, are now able to afford treatments for common illnesses.

—Kristina Trajkov & the Malamulo Cookbook Team

ABOUT MALAMULO HOSPITAL

Malamulo Hospital has been providing health care to one of the poorest districts in Malawi, Africa, since 1902. It is located 65 kilometers (about 40 miles) southeast of the city of Blantyre in Thyolo District in the southern part of Malawi. The hospital serves a catchment population of 129,000 from two surrounding districts, which are among the poorest in Africa, with many locals earning an average income of less than $1 per day. The hospital has a bed capacity of 275. A number of activities are implemented with assistance from both local and international donors, such as HIV testing and counseling, youth-friendly health services, home-based care, nutrition awareness, infection prevention promotion, and family planning. The hospital also runs 15 mobile sites with three outpatient clinics that operate on a daily basis.

Until recently, Malamulo Hospital has been able to provide the health care needed to children under the age of five with no cost to the patient's family. A Malawi government initiative reimbursed the hospital any costs for basic services accessed by these children. However, these reimbursements have not been coming through to Malamulo Hospital recently, leaving the patient's family to cover the costs for their medical care.

Your purchase of this cookbook supports these services, enabling us to continue to provide much-needed medical help to Malawi's children. All proceeds of this cookbook directly impact the lives of our patients.

MALAMULO
HOSPITAL
MALAMULOHOSPITAL.ORG

CONTENTS

BACK TO BASICS

GNOCCHI

BASIC EGG NOODLES

BASIC TOMATO SAUCE

FRESH BASIL PESTO

NEVER FAIL OIL CRUST

HOMEMADE YOGURT

GNOCCHI

1 cup flour
1/2 teaspoon salt
1/8 teaspoon pepper
1/2 cup mashed potato
3 tablespoons margarine/butter, melted
6 cups water

Combine flour and pepper in a bowl. In separate bowl mix margarine/butter and potato until creamy. Gradually add flour and mix well until combined. Turn out onto lightly floured surface and knead for 4 minutes. Form dough into 1 inch balls and indent each ball lightly with a fork. In a large saucepan, bring water to boil. Place balls in boiling water and cook for 5 minutes or until all balls float to the top. Drain water and top with favorite sauce.

BASIC EGG NOODLES

1 egg, beaten
2 tablespoons milk
1 cup flour
1/2 teaspoon salt

Mix flour and salt in a bowl and form well in the center. Mix egg and milk together and pour into well; combine slowly with fork working toward the perimeter of the bowl. As the dough stiffens, use your hands to continue mixing. Roll dough out into a very thin sheet on a lightly floured surface and let stand for a few minutes. Cut into desired pasta shapes. Cook immediately or dry for future use.

BASIC TOMATO SAUCE

10 cups tomatoes, peeled and diced
1 tablespoon oil
1 tablespoon salt
Boiling water

Score tomatoes as shown in photo and place in boiling water for 2 minutes, then peel. Heat oil and add tomatoes and salt. Simmer until desired texture.

Can be canned or frozen.

FRESH BASIL PESTO

1 cup fresh basil leaves, packed
1/4 cup extra virgin olive oil
1/4 cup pine nuts or cashew or macadamia nuts
2 medium sized garlic cloves, minced
Salt and freshly ground black pepper to taste

Blend basil, nuts, and garlic, scraping down sides occasionally, until almost smooth. With blender running, add oil in a slow, steady stream and continue to combine. Transfer to a bowl. Season with salt and pepper. Stir to combine.

HOMEMADE YOGURT

4 1/4 cups whole milk
3 tablespoons yogurt

Pour the milk into a saucepan and let it heat. When it begins to steam, remove it from the heat and transfer it into a glass or earthenware bowl. Do not use stainless steel. Allow the milk to cool down until it's just warm: check that it has cooled to the right temperature by feeling the side of the bowl with your hands. Then spoon in the yogurt and cover with tea towel. Leave it overnight to rest. The next morning, the yogurt should look like white firm custard. Place a cheesecloth or muslin cloth into a sieve, with a bowl placed underneath, and ladle the yogurt into the cloth and allow it to strain. As the draining process will take several hours, it's best to transfer it into the fridge. Serve when your yogurt has reached the consistency that you wish. It can be enjoyed plain, with nuts or honey, fruit, or even be used for the base for sauces like tzatziki.

NEVER-FAIL OIL CRUST

2 cups of white flour (or 1 white/1 whole wheat or 2 cups whole wheat)
2 tablespoon oats or wheat germ
1 teaspoon salt
1/2 cup oil
1/2 cup ice-cold water

With fork mix together first three ingredients. Combine oil and cold water in a separate container, mixing well; add all at once to flour mixture. Stir just until flour is dampened. Divide into two balls. Roll out each bowl between two sheets of wax paper or clear plastic wrap until size for crust. Bake in 220°C/430°F oven for 10 minutes until brown for a premade pie shell for glaze or cream pie—or put in pie filling before baking. For pie with covering, place second pie crust on top of filling, then bake according to pie filling directions.

Makes 2 crusts.

BREADS

WHOLE-WHEAT BREAD

5 cups warm water
2 tablespoons dry yeast
6 tablespoons sugar (brown or white)
4 teaspoons salt
2/3 cup oil
6 cups white flour
6 cups whole-wheat flour

Place water, yeast, and sugar in a bowl or mixer. Stir and let sit for 5 to 10 minutes. Add oil, salt, and half of the flour and beat well. Slowly knead or mix in remaining flour, one cup at a time. Dough should be slightly sticky but easily rub off hands. Knead for 5 minutes. Place in large bowl, oil top of dough, and cover. Let dough rise until double. Divide dough into 5 even pieces or shape the dough into dinner rolls or burger or hotdog rolls. Shape into loaves by flattening each piece and folding the corners of the dough to bring everything to the center. Place in greased pans and let rise until double. Place in 180°C/350°F oven and bake loaf until brown and sounds hollow when tapped. Baking time is dependent on the oven—can be 20 to 50 minutes. Remove from oven and pan and let cool; cover with cloth.

VARIATIONS

add sunflower, pumpkin, sesame, and/or flax seeds

add 1/2 to 2 cups of oats, decreasing flour as needed

add 1/2 to 1 cup local cornmeal, decreasing flour as needed

cinnamon raisin—increase sugar to 1/2 to 3/4 cup, add 1 to 2 tablespoons cinnamon and 1 to 2 cups of raisins; combine with flours

onion—chop two medium onions and sauté them. After cooling, add to dough with a little dry flour. Can add any herbs of choice, including 1 tablespoon of dill, if desired.

tomato basil—1 cup dried tomatoes and fresh or dried basil

FLOUR TORTILLAS

2 cups white flour
1/2 teaspoon salt
3/4 cup hot water
2 tablespoons oil

Mix first two ingredients, then add water and oil. Knead dough for a few minutes. Take golf ball-size pieces of dough and roll out into a thin circle on floured board or counter. Place on hot, dry (no oil) fry pan on medium heat and cook on each side until bubbles form and dough browns up in spots. Eat with beans and toppings like burritos or with curry like a chapatti.

PITA BREAD

1 1/8 cups warm water
1 1/2 teaspoons yeast
1 teaspoon salt
1 tablespoon oil
1 1/2 teaspoons sugar
1 1/2 cups flour
1 1/2 cups whole-wheat flour

Knead dough in bread machine, Kitchen Aid, or Bosch for 10 minutes or by hand or until well kneaded. Roll into a 12" rope and cut into 8 to 10 pieces. Roll each piece into a ball and, using a rolling pin, roll each ball into a 6 to 7" circle. Place each circle onto a floured surface to rise covered for 30 minutes, or until slightly puffy. Preheat oven to 265°C/500°F. Place 2 to 3 pitas on a wire rack and then into the oven for 4 to 5 minutes until the dough has puffed up and is slightly golden. Remove from the oven and cover with a damp kitchen cloth.

EASY CORNBREAD

1 cup flour
1 cup cornmeal or local corn flour
1/4 cup sugar
1/4 cup oil
4 teaspoons baking powder
3/4 teaspoon salt
2 eggs
1 cup milk or water

Combine all ingredients and mix well. Place in greased pan. Bake for approximately 20 to 30 minutes in 180°C/350°F oven, until slightly brown on top and toothpick comes out clean.

GARLIC NAAN

1 1/2 teaspoons yeast
1 cup warm water
2 tablespoons sugar
3 tablespoons milk
1 egg, lightly beaten
2 teaspoons salt
4 cups flour
2 teaspoons garlic, minced
1/4 cup melted butter

Mix water and yeast until dissolved. Add sugar, milk, egg, salt, and flour. Knead 10 minutes. Form into 20 golf ball-size balls and let rise 30 minutes. On heated, oiled grill place rolled out bread pieces and brush with butter and garlic mixture. Turn after 2 minutes and brush other side with butter. Remove from heat when cooked (about 2 minutes each side). Sprinkle with fresh coriander for garnish.

ITALIAN BREAD

1 tablespoon yeast
2 cups warm water
2 tablespoons sugar
2 teaspoons salt
4 1/2 cups white flour, plus 1 additional cup

Dissolve yeast in water, then add sugar, salt, and flour. Mix well and leave in mixing bowl. Let dough rise until double. Now add up to 1 more cup white flour. Knead well, until dough no longer sticks to your hands. Divide dough and roll out to desired shape. Place on greased baking pan. Allow to rise again. Bake in 200°C/390°F oven for 40 minutes or until golden brown.

GARLIC BREADSTICKS

2 cups warm water
2 tablespoons yeast
2 tablespoons sugar
1 tablespoons salt
1/4 cup oil
6 cups flour
1/4 to 1/2 cup margarine
4 large garlic cloves, minced

Mix all ingredients, adding last few cups of flour slowly. Knead well at least 5 minutes. Place dough in a greased bowl, turn greased side up, and let rise covered for 45 minutes or until doubled in size. After dough rises, take small pieces of dough and shape into bread sticks. With knife, make 1 or 2 slits down middle of stick lengthwise. Allow dough to rise to double on the cookie sheet. Melt margarine and mix in garlic. After dough has risen, spread garlic margarine on breadsticks and place in 190°C/370°F oven, baking until golden brown on top and bottom.

PIZZA DOUGH

2 cups warm water
2 tablespoons yeast
2 tablespoons sugar
1 tablespoon salt
1/4 cup oil
6 cups of flour

Mix all ingredients, adding last few cups of flour slowly. Knead well for at least 5 minutes. Allow dough to rise for 5 to 10 minutes. Roll out crusts on large cookie sheet until very thin. Place desired toppings on and bake at 220°C/430°F for 20 to 25 minutes until brown on bottom and cheese is browning on top.

Makes 3 crusts.

BANANA BREAD

2 cups whole-wheat flour
1 cup sugar
1 teaspoon salt
1 teaspoon baking soda
1/2 cup oil
2 eggs
3 large ripe bananas, mashed
1 teaspoon vanilla
3 tablespoons (or as needed) soy milk or water
1 cup chopped walnuts (optional)

Preheat oven to 180°C/350°F. With a wooden spoon, mix oil into the mashed bananas in a large mixing bowl. Mix in the sugar, eggs, vanilla, and walnuts. Sprinkle the baking soda and salt over the mixture and mix in. Add the flour last, mix. Add water/milk as required. Pour mixture into a buttered loaf pan. Bake for 1 hour. Cool on a rack. Remove from pan and slice to serve.

CINNAMON RAISIN BAGELS

1 1/2 cups lukewarm water
1/4 cup packed brown sugar, additional 3 tablespoons
2 tablespoons honey
4 teaspoons yeast
4 teaspoons cinnamon
1 cup raisins
1 1/4 cups flour, additional 3 to 4 cups flour
1/2 teaspoon salt, additional 1 teaspoon salt
1 teaspoon baking soda

Whisk water, sugar, honey, and yeast until yeast dissolves. Stir in the 1 1/4 cup of flour, salt, cinnamon, and raisins. Then begin adding the additional flour while kneading the dough for 8 to 10 minutes. The dough will be sticky when done kneading. Divide dough in half, then half again, and then those into fourths. Roll between palms until dough becomes fat sticks of 1/2 inch by 6 to 7 inches long. Join the ends by pinching and twisting to close the circles. Put 3 tablespoons of sugar, 1 teaspoon salt, and 1 teaspoon baking soda to boil in a large pot of water. Add 3 to 4 bagels at a time and boil for 1 minute on each side. Place boiled bagels on a towel and when all finished boiling, place on oiled cookie sheet and into a preheated oven at 140°C/280°F. Bake on each side for 5 to 8 minutes or until golden brown.

SAVORY BAGELS

1 1/2 cups lukewarm water
1/4 cup packed brown sugar, additional 3 tablespoons
2 tablespoons honey
4 teaspoons yeast
1 1/4 cups flour, additional 3 to 4 cups flour
1/2 teaspoon salt, additional 2 teaspoons salt
2 small onions, diced
1 teaspoon baking soda

Sauté onions with 1 teaspoon salt until clear on color in low heat stirring often, and set aside. Whisk water, sugar, honey, and yeast until yeast dissolves. Stir in the 1 1/4 cups of flour, onions, and salt. Then begin adding the additional flour while kneading the dough for 8 to 10 minutes. The dough will be sticky when done kneading. Divide dough in half, then half again, and then those into fourths. Roll between palms until dough becomes fat sticks of 1/2 inch by 6 to 7 inches long. Join the ends by pinching and twisting to close the circles. Put 3 tablespoons of sugar, 1 teaspoon salt, and 1 teaspoon baking soda to boil in a large pot of water. Add 3 to 4 bagels at a time and boil for 1 minute on each side. Place boiled bagels on a towel and when all finished boiling, place on oiled cookie sheet and into a preheated oven at 140°C/280°F. Bake on each side for 5 to 8 minutes or until golden brown.

SNACKS & STARTERS

BRUSCHETTA

4 medium tomatoes, diced
1/3 cup chopped fresh basil
1/3 cup chopped fresh parsley
2 garlic cloves, finely chopped
1/2 teaspoon each salt and pepper
1/3 cup olive oil
8 1/2-inch-thick slices of crusty Italian or French bread

Preheat oven to 200°C/390°F. Combine all ingredients except bread and set aside. Place bread slices on a cookie sheet and toast in the oven for 5 minutes. Flip slices and toast for 5 more minutes or until golden brown. Remove and place on a serving plate. Spoon tomato mixture over toasted bread and serve immediately.

TORTILLA CHIPS

2 cups white flour
1/2 teaspoon salt
3/4 cup hot water
2 tablespoons oil

Mix first two ingredients, then add water and oil. Knead dough for a few minutes. Take golf ball-size pieces of dough and roll out into thin circles on floured board or counter, then slice into wedges and place on slightly greased cookie sheet. Bake at 180°C/350°F until crisp. Then fry wedges in hot oil and drain on a paper towel. Season chips while still warm.

FRESH SALSA

6 tomatoes, diced
1 medium onion, finely diced
2 to 3 tablespoons jalapeno pepper, diced very small
2 garlic cloves, minced
1/4 cup fresh coriander
Salt to taste

Combine all ingredients and serve with corn chips or tortilla chips.

EMPANADAS

1 cup white flour, additional 1/4 cup
1/2 cup margarine or butter
1/4 cup ice-cold water
1/4 teaspoon salt
Ground veggie meat of choice
Onion
Green pepper
Garlic
Salt
Olive oil

Chop up onions, green pepper, and garlic. Sauté in pan with a little olive oil. Add ground veggie meat to pan of sautéed veggies. Season to taste. In a large mixing bowl, cut flour, salt, and margarine together with fork. Add ice-cold water a little at a time while mixing together. Mix just until dough comes together. Roll dough out on floured surface. Using a cookie cutter or round cup, cut into 4 to 5 inch circles. Spoon 2 tablespoon portions of filling onto each circle and fold in half. Crimp edges together with fork. Place on baking sheet and bake at 180°C/350°F until crust is golden brown.

FALAFEL

2 cups cooked chickpeas
1 cup onion
2 tablespoons parsley, finely chopped
2 tablespoons coriander, finely chopped
1 teaspoon salt
1/2 to 1 teaspoon chili powder
4 garlic cloves
1 teaspoon cumin
1 teaspoon baking powder
4 to 6 tablespoons flour

Blend onion, parsley, coriander, salt, chili, cumin, and garlic. Add chickpeas and pulse. Add baking powder and flour and blend until combined. Form into a ball, adding more flour if dough sticks to the hand. Refrigerate for 1 to 2 hours. Form into walnut-size balls and fry, turning when browned on each side.

OATMEAL PATTIES

2 cups oats
2 eggs, slightly beaten
3/4 cup milk
1 teaspoon salt
1/4 teaspoon dried sage
1 small chopped onion
1 garlic clove, mashed

Mix all ingredients together. Let stand for 30 minutes or until absorbed. Form into patties and fry in oil.

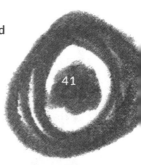

41

BUTTERNUT SQUASH SOUP

2 medium butternut squash, peeled, seeded, and cubed
2 tablespoons olive oil
3 teaspoons curry powder
3 teaspoons salt
1 teaspoon black pepper
1 teaspoon cinnamon
1 teaspoon nutmeg
1 large brown onion
2 tablespoons butter
2 tablespoons flour
2 crushed garlic cloves
2 to 3 cups vegetable broth
1 cup water
1 cup milk

Toss squash in olive oil, 2 teaspoons of curry powder, 1 teaspoon sea salt, black pepper, cinnamon, and nutmeg and roast in a moderate oven until tender. Puree in blender until smooth. Sauté onion in butter with salt until tender in large pot. Add flour, remaining curry powder, and garlic and cook a few minutes. Whisk in vegetable broth and keep stirring while sauce thickens. Season to taste and set aside. Add squash puree. Add water and milk; simmer for approximately 1 hour on low heat. Garnish with fresh coriander.

CRACKERS

2 cups whole-wheat flour
1/3 cup butter (softened or melted)
1 teaspoon salt
1/2 cup warm water, more or less as needed

Preheat oven to 180°C/350°F. Mix dry ingredients with a whisk. Add butter and mix until evenly distributed (will appear dry or a little lumpy). Add water as needed. Knead into non-sticky dough. Roll out on a floured surface. Use cookie cutters or knife to create the desired shape. Bake about 20 minutes or until edges are browned.

EGGPLANT DIP

2 cups eggplant, chopped in 1/2 inch cubes
2 teaspoons salt
2 tablespoons oil
3 garlic cloves
2 tablespoons lemon juice
2 tablespoons parsley
1/4 cup plain yogurt (optional)

Place eggplant in bowl together with salt and oil, mix well, and let sit for 30 minutes. Preheat oven to 180°C/350 °F and then roast eggplant until tender and slightly browning. Once slightly cooled, process eggplant together with garlic, lemon juice, parsley, and yogurt. If you don't have yogurt, add water until smooth. Add salt and pepper to taste.

SIMPLE HUMMUS

1/2 cup chickpeas
2 garlic cloves, minced
4 tablespoons lemon juice
1/2 teaspoon salt
1/3 cup water
1 tablespoon parsley, finely chopped (optional)
1/4 teaspoon paprika
2 tablespoons oil

Soak chickpeas overnight and cook them in the same water until tender. Drain the chickpeas and mash with fork or blend chickpeas with garlic, lemon juice, water, and parsley until smooth. Place in serving bowl and sprinkle with paprika, then dribble oil over.

GUACAMOLE

1 large avocado, peeled, mashed
2 garlic cloves
2 teaspoons lemon juice
2 tablespoons fresh coriander, minced (optional)
1 large tomato, diced
1 small onion, finely diced
1 teaspoon salt

Add avocado, garlic, and lemon juice in a bowl and mash until smooth. Stir in remainder of ingredients.

RED LENTIL SOUP

1 tablespoon oil
2 medium onions, finely chopped
1 1/2 cups red lentils, rinsed
6 cups of water
1 tablespoon McKay's beef-style seasoning
1 bay leaf
1 teaspoon salt
1/8 teaspoon pepper
1 teaspoon dried dill
1/2 teaspoon dried parsley
1 to 2 tablespoons tomato paste

In large pot, heat oil, then sauté onions. Once onions are soft, add the lentils and stir for several minutes. Add the remaining ingredients and bring to boil. Simmer until lentils are very soft, about 35 minutes. Serve hot.

MAINS

MEXICAN RICE

NUTTY CABBAGE STIR FRY

CHICKPEAS & GREENS WITH
MOROCCAN SPICES

CHICKPEA STEW WITH EGG
DUMPLINGS

BOBOTIE PIE

VEGGIE QUICHE

SPICY OKRA

OKRA WITH TOMATOES

NUTTY RED KIDNEY BEAN STEW

SPINACH BAKE

MEXICAN EGGS

PEAS & EGGS

PANCIT BIHON

GREEN BEANS & TOMATOES

SPICY REFRIED BEANS

LENTIL PASTA SAUCE

ASIAN GREEN BEANS

FRIED RICE

EGGPLANT ADOBO

BENGAN MASALA

MEXICAN RICE

2 tablespoons vegetable oil
1 onion, chopped
1 teaspoon minced garlic
1 teaspoon chili powder
1 tablespoon ground cumin
1 cup uncooked short-grain white rice
1 3/4 cups veggie broth
1/4 cup tomato paste

Preheat oven to 180°C/350°F. Heat the oil in a large skillet over medium heat. Add the onion and garlic; cook and stir until onion is translucent. Stir in the chili powder and cumin and cook for about 30 seconds. Add the rice, veggie chicken broth, and tomato paste and bring to a boil. Transfer to a 1 quart casserole dish and cover with aluminum foil or a lid. Bake for 35 to 40 minutes or until liquid has been absorbed and rice is tender. Let rest for 3 to 5 minutes before serving.

NUTTY CABBAGE STIR FRY

5 cups thinly sliced cabbage
1 cup chopped peanuts
1 tablespoon chopped onions
1 tablespoon sesame seeds
1 tablespoon sesame oil
Salt to taste
1 teaspoon chopped ginger (optional)
2 teaspoons sugar (optional)

Heat oil. Add rest of the ingredients together. Stir and toss over medium heat till cabbage is cooked yet crisp. Serve with rice.

CHICKPEAS & GREENS WITH MOROCCAN SPICES

1 large bunch of chard, stems removed, chopped
3 cups cooked chickpeas
6 garlic cloves, coarsely chopped
2 teaspoons sweet paprika
1 teaspoon whole black peppercorns
1 1/2 teaspoons ground cumin
1/2 teaspoon turmeric
3 tablespoons olive oil
1/4 cup cilantro, chopped
2 tablespoons parsley, chopped
1 white onion, chopped
1 bell pepper, diced into 1/2 inch squares
1/4 teaspoon dried thyme
1 small dried red chili
4 tomatoes, peeled, seeded, and diced
Salt to taste

Mince garlic with 1/2 teaspoon salt until smooth. Add the dried spices, 1 teaspoon oil to moisten the mixture, and 2 tablespoons of the cilantro and parsley. Heat the remaining oil in a large skillet over medium-high heat. Add the onion, pepper, thyme, and dried chili. Cook for 7 minutes, then stir in the garlic paste mixture, chickpeas, and 1/2 cup water or bean broth. When the onion is soft, add the tomatoes, greens, 1/2 teaspoon salt, and another 1/2 cup water. Reduce the heat to low and simmer for 5 minutes. Stir in the remaining cilantro and serve.

CHICKPEA STEW WITH EGG DUMPLINGS

FOR STEW

4 cups cooked chickpeas
4 cups water
1 small onion, chopped
2 tablespoons margarine or butter
1 tablespoon flour
1/2 teaspoon dried basil
1 teaspoon salt

FOR DUMPLINGS

1 cup water
4 tablespoons butter
1/2 teaspoon salt
1 1/3 cups flour
4 eggs

For stew: Sauté chopped onions in butter/margarine. Add flour and salt and stir until slightly golden. Add chickpeas, water, and basil. Bring to a boil. For dumplings: Bring water, butter, and salt to a boil. Remove from heat. Add flour all at once and stir until blended. Add eggs one at a time, stirring well after each one. Drop by spoonfuls into boiling stew. Reduce heat to simmer. Cover and cook for 20 minutes.

BOBOTIE PIE

2 tablespoons butter
1 onion, thinly sliced
1 tablespoon vinegar
1 teaspoon curry powder
1 teaspoon salt
1 teaspoon sugar
1 cup cooked lentils
1 tablespoon chutney
2 eggs, slightly beaten
3/4 cup milk
1 slice of bread
1 uncooked pastry shell

Soak bread in milk. Sauté onion in butter until soft, then add curry, sugar, salt, and vinegar, chutney, and lentils. Drain milk from bread (save milk) and mash with fork. Add to sautéed mixture and stir in one beaten egg. Pour all of this into pastry. Beat 2nd egg, add milk saved from bread, and pour over top of lentil mixture. Dot with butter and bake at 200°C/390°F for 25 to 30 minutes.

VEGGIE QUICHE

1/3 cup onion, minced
6 eggs, beaten
1/4 teaspoon salt
1/4 teaspoon garlic salt
1/2 cup shredded carrot
1/2 cup spinach
1/2 to 1 cup mushrooms (optional)
1 1/2 cups milk
1/4 teaspoon pepper
2 cups flour
2/3 cup cold butter/margarine
1/2 teaspoon salt
4 to 7 tablespoons ice-cold water

Mix flour and salt together using a fork, then cut in butter/margarine until mixture resembles coarse crumbs. Sprinkle 1 tablespoon cold water over part of mixture and toss with a fork. Push moistened dough to side of bowl. Repeat using 1 tablespoon at a time until all dough is moistened but not too sticky. On lightly floured surface, roll out dough to size of pie tin and transfer into pie tin. Bake at 230°C/445°F for 12 minutes, then remove from oven. Reduce heat to 180°C/350°F. In a bowl, mix carrot, onion, mushrooms, and spinach and place in crust. Then combine eggs, milk, salt, pepper, and garlic salt. Pour over vegetable mix and bake at 180°C/350°F for 40 minutes.

SPICY OKRA

4 cups young okra, trimmed and left whole
2 tablespoons oil
1 to 2 teaspoons chili flakes
2 garlic cloves, peeled and cut into long slices
1 1/2 to 2 tablespoons soy sauce
1 teaspoon oriental sesame oil (optional)
Pinch of sugar

Wipe off the okra with a damp cloth and leave to dry in a single layer. Put the oil in a frying pan and set over medium-high heat. When it is hot, add the garlic and chili flakes. Now toss in the okra and cook until it turns bright green, 1 to 2 minutes. Turn the heat down to low and continue cooking, with the pan uncovered, for another 10 to 15 minutes, until the okra is tender. You will need to stir or shake the pan every now and then. Finally, add the soy sauce, sesame oil, and sugar. Cook and stir another 2 to 3 minutes. Serve hot.

OKRA WITH TOMATOES

2 tablespoons oil
3 cups fresh okra, tops and tails removed and then
cut crosswise into 1/4 inch-thick rounds
3 medium tomatoes, peeled, and chopped
3 medium garlic cloves, peeled, and mashed to a pulp
3 tablespoons fresh lime or lemon juice
1/2 teaspoon ground coriander
1/2 teaspoon ground cumin
1/8 to 1/4 teaspoon cayenne
3/4 teaspoon salt, or to taste
Freshly ground black pepper to taste

Put the oil in a large, preferably nonstick, frying pan and set over medium-high heat. When
hot, put in the cut okra. Stir and fry for 7 to 10 minutes. When the okra starts to brown,
turn the heat down to medium and cook, stirring, for another 3 to 4 minutes. The okra will
have browned a bit more. Turn the heat down to low and cook 2 to 3 minutes, or until the
okra is almost tender. Now put in all the remaining ingredients. Stir gently and cook on low
heat for 4 to 5 minutes, or until all the flavors have melded and the tomatoes have dried a
little. Check for salt adding more if you need it.

NUTTY RED KIDNEY BEAN STEW

1 1/2 cups dried red kidney beans
2 teaspoons salt, or to taste
3 tablespoons peanut or canola oil
1 medium onion, peeled, finely chopped
2 garlic cloves, peeled, finely chopped
1 teaspoon ground cumin
1 cup tomato sauce
1/4 teaspoon cayenne
1 tablespoon fresh lemon juice
1 1/2 tablespoons smooth peanut butter

Soak and cook beans. Do not drain. Add the salt to the beans, stir to mix, and leave the beans in their cooking liquid. Put the oil in a wide, medium pot and set over medium heat. Add the onion, garlic, and pepper. Stir and fry just until the onion has turned translucent, turning the heat down as needed. Add the cumin and stir once. Put in the tomato sauce, cayenne, lemon juice, and 1/2 cup of water. Stir and bring to a simmer. Turn the heat down to low and simmer gently, stirring now and then, for 15 minutes. Meanwhile, put the peanut butter in a small bowl. Slowly add about 6 tablespoons of cooking liquid from the beans, mixing as you go. Stir this mixture back into the pot of beans. When the tomato mixture has finished cooking, pour it into the pot of beans as well. Stir and bring to a simmer. Cover, turn the heat down to low, and simmer gently for 10 minutes, stirring occasionally. Serve hot.

SPINACH BAKE

1 tablespoon butter
2 cups cooked rice
4 cups cooked spinach (Swiss chard)
1 cup grated carrot
1 large onion
3 to 4 small bell peppers/capsicums
2 eggs, beaten
2 tablespoons McKay's chicken-style seasoning
1 teaspoon garlic salt
Salt and pepper to taste

Preheat oven to 180°C/350°F. Sauté onion and bell peppers in butter until tender. In a large mixing bowl, combine all ingredients and mix together. Pour out into a large baking dish and bake for 45 minutes to 1 hour.

MEXICAN EGGS

1 packet corn chips
4 poached eggs
2 cups refried beans
2 cups marinara sauce
2 ripe avocados
Coriander
Salt and pepper to taste

Arrange corn chips on plate. Spread 1/2 cup of beans over the chips, top with 1/2 cup of marinara sauce, place poached egg on sauce, and splay 1/2 avocado on top of egg. Sprinkle with coriander for garnish.

PEAS & EGGS

1 small onion, minced
6 garlic cloves, minced
1 cup green peas, cooked
Salt to taste
2 eggs
Black/white pepper to taste
1 tablespoon oil
1 tablespoon McKay's chicken-style seasoning

Heat pan on the stove and add oil. In a separate bowl, beat the eggs. Add spices if desired. When oil is hot, put in 1/2 of garlic and cook until slightly brown. Add onions and a pinch of salt. Cook until slightly brown around the edges. Pour the eggs into the pan and let them spread to cover the base of the pan. Flip to cook the other side. Once it's cooked, remove from pan and set aside. In the same pan, add oil and cook remaining onions and garlic as above. Add green peas and cook for about 3 minutes. Slice egg patty into small squares or strips and add into the green pea mixture. Add salt, chicken-style seasoning, and spices to taste. Let simmer for 5 to 10 minutes. Serve warm with rice.

PANCIT BIHON

1 pack (250g) rice noodles
Soy sauce
Salt to taste
4 eggs, beaten
2 tablespoons oil
Black pepper/white pepper
4 garlic cloves, minced
1 medium-sized onion, finely diced
4 cups cabbage, sliced into thin strips
2 cups green beans, sliced into thin slants
2 small carrots, jullienned
Water or broth

Soak rice noodles in water for 5 minutes, then cut to 5 to 6 inches length (or shorter if so desired). Drain noodles. Sprinkle soy sauce into noodles until evenly light brown. Set aside. Heat oil in a pan. Sauté 1/2 of the onion and garlic until brown. Sprinkle salt. Add beaten eggs and scramble until cooked. Remove from heat. Sauté the rest of the onion and garlic until slightly brown. Add salt. Add carrots and green beans and sauté until cooked but still crisp. Add cabbage and scrambled eggs. Cook for about 2 minutes. Add 1/2 cup broth or water and cook until boiling. Add rice noodles and stir until well mixed with the veggies. Salt to taste. Serve with a slice of lemon.

GREEN BEANS & TOMATOES

2 cups of green beans, washed, with tips removed
2 cups water
1 cup tomatoes, diced
1 tablespoon McKay's chicken-style seasoning
1 onion, diced
3 garlic cloves
2 tablespoons oil
2 to 3 tablespoons cornstarch
1 cup water
Salt to taste

Boil green beans until cooked with bright green color. Remove beans from water and arrange on a serving dish. In a pan, sauté garlic and onions until slightly brown. Add tomatoes, salt, and seasoning. Simmer for 5 minutes. Dissolve cornstarch in water. Add cornstarch mixture to the sauce. Let simmer for 5 more minutes. Serve warm with rice.

SPICY REFRIED BEANS

1 medium onion, diced
1 carrot, grated
1 zucchini, grated
2 tablespoons oil
1/2 teaspoon salt
2 garlic cloves, minced
1 cup tomato sauce
1 cup beans, cooked, mashed
Chili powder to taste
1 teaspoon of McKay's chicken-style or beef-style seasoning

Heat oil in frypan and sauté onion together with garlic and salt until slightly brown. Add carrots and zucchini, then sauté for 2 minutes. Add beans and tomato sauce and simmer for 5 minutes. Add seasoning and chili powder, allow to simmer for another 2 minutes, and serve hot with tortilla wraps.

LENTIL PASTA SAUCE

1 medium onion, diced
1 carrot, grated
2 tablespoons oil
1/2 teaspoon salt
2 garlic cloves, minced
2 cups tomato sauce
1 cup red lentils, washed
1 cup water
2 teaspoons of McKay's chicken-style or beef-style seasoning

Heat oil in frypan and sauté onion together with garlic and salt until slightly brown. Add carrots, then sauté for 2 minutes. Add lentils, water, and tomato sauce and simmer for 10 minutes or until lentils are tender. Add seasoning and allow to simmer for another 2 minutes. Serve with pasta.

ASIAN GREEN BEANS

4 cups green beans, washed, with tips removed
6 cups water
4 tablespoons soy sauce
4 garlic cloves
2 tablespoons oil

In large saucepan, bring water to boil, then add green beans to boil for about 5 minutes until cooked but still crisp. Remove from hot water and place under running cold water until cooled. Then in frypan, heat oil and sauté garlic until it starts to brown. Add green beans together with soy sauce and sauté for about 2 to 3 minutes. Garnish with sesame seeds.

FRIED RICE

2 cups cold cooked rice
1 medium onion, diced
1 carrot, chopped
2 tablespoons oil
1/2 teaspoon ginger
2 tablespoons soy sauce
3 garlic cloves, minced
1 cup cooked peas
1 cup cabbage, shredded
2 eggs, lightly beaten
1/2 teaspoon salt

Sauté ginger and garlic in hot oil for 30 seconds, then add vegetables, except peas, and sauté until tender. Add rice and peas and mix well. In a small bowl, mix together the eggs and soy sauce. Make a well in the rice and pour egg mixture in. Allow the egg to cook until nearly dry, then mix the egg and rice mixture together. Serve hot.

EGGPLANT ADOBO

2 cups eggplant, sliced into 1 to 2 inch squares about 1/2 inch thin
1 cup potatoes, peeled and chopped into 1/2 inch pieces
1 medium onion, diced
2 to 3 garlic cloves
3 tablespoons oil
3 tablespoons soy sauce
2 tablespoons lemon juice
2 tablespoons sugar
Salt to taste
Freshly ground Black pepper to taste
Cayenne pepper to taste
1 bay leaf
2 cups water
2 to 3 tablespoons cornstarch
1/4 cup water

Place eggplant in bowl and add 2 teaspoons of salt and 2 tablespoons of oil. Oven or pan fry eggplant and potato pieces until slightly brown. Set aside. Sauté onions and garlic until brown. Add all the ingredients except cornstarch mixture and simmer for 15 minutes. Add fried eggplant and potato pieces. Simmer for 5 to 10 minutes. Add cornstarch mixture and cook for 3 minutes. Remove bay leaf. Serve with rice.

BENGAN MASALA

3 to 4 garlic cloves, minced
1 inch ginger, minced
2 to 3 tablespoons oil
2 onions, finely diced
1/2 teaspoon cumin seeds
1/2 teaspoon cayenne
1/4 teaspoon turmeric
1 teaspoon coriander powder
1 teaspoon garam masala
3 to 4 tomatoes, diced
6 to 8 cups eggplant, finely diced
1 teaspoon salt

Heat oil in frypan and brown garlic and ginger. Then sauté onions until slightly browned. Add spices and sauté for a few minutes. Add tomatoes and eggplant and simmer until eggplant is soft, then add salt. Serve hot with rice.

DESSERTS

FROZEN BANANA TREATS

6 bananas
Honey
Crushed nuts or coconut

Coat bananas with honey. Sprinkle on nuts or coconut. Place on tray and freeze.

PASSION FRUIT PIE

1 can dessert cream
1 can sweetened condensed milk
10g kosher gelatin, unflavored
1 1/4 cup hot water
3 to 4 passion fruits
1 baked pie crust

Mix filling ingredients together in blender and pour into crust and chill for 3 to 4 hours. Serve cold.

PUMPKIN PIE

4 eggs
3 cups pumpkin or squash, mashed or blended, drained and cooked
1 1/2 cups sugar (white or brown)
1 teaspoon salt
2 teaspoons cinnamon
1 teaspoon ginger
1/2 teaspoon cloves
3 cups milk

Combine all ingredients and mix well. Pour into two pie crusts. Place in a 220°C/430°F oven for 15 minutes. Then turn down oven to 180°C/350°F. Bake an additional 40 to 50 minutes until knife inserted in center comes out clean. Cool and serve.

CARROT CAKE

1 cup sugar
2 cups whole-wheat flour
1 teaspoon salt
2 teaspoons cinnamon
1 teaspoon baking soda
1 cup oil
3 cups raw carrots, grated
1 cup nuts, chopped (optional)

Preheat oven to 180°C/350°F. Mix together dry ingredients, then make a well in center of mixture, add the oil and carrots, and mix well. Pour mixture into a well-greased pan and bake for 40 minutes or until toothpick or skewer inserted comes out clean.

MANGO & BANANA SORBET

2 cups banana, peeled and sliced
1 1/2 cups mangoes, peeled, deseeded, and chopped
1/4 cup fruit juice

Place banana and mango in freezer overnight. Then in a processor or blender, add the banana and mango together with the fruit juice and process until smooth.

FRUIT CRISP

4 cups fruit (apples, guavas, mangoes, peaches, etc., chopped—fresh or canned—or
    just mulberries or strawberries if you have available)
2/3 cup brown sugar
1/2 cup flour
1/2 cup oats
3/4 teaspoon cinnamon
1/8 teaspoon salt
1/3 cup margarine, softened

OPTIONAL
Add 1/2 to 1 teaspoon nutmeg
For berries—add 1 to 2 teaspoon lemon juice

Layer fruit in the bottom of the baking pan. Mix together all other ingredients and sprinkle over top of the fruit. Bake in 190° to 200°C/370° to 390°F oven until topping is light brown, about 30 to 50 minutes depending on oven and size of pan. (Fruit should have bubbled up throughout while baking.) Enjoy warm or cool, with ice cream or cream if desired.

COCOA OATMEAL COOKIES

1 cup butter, softened
1 cup brown sugar, packed
2 eggs
1 teaspoon vanilla extract
1 1/2 cups all-purpose flour
1/3 cup unsweetened cocoa powder (or carob powder)
1 teaspoon baking soda
1/2 teaspoon salt
3 cups rolled oats

Preheat oven to 180ºC/350ºF. Beat butter (or margarine) and sugar until creamy. Add eggs and vanilla; beat well. Add combined flour, cocoa powder, baking soda, and salt; mix well. Stir in oats; mix well. Drop dough by rounded tablespoonfuls onto ungreased cookie sheets. Bake 10 to 12 minutes until cookies are almost set. Do not overbake. Cool 1 minute on cookies sheets, then move to wire racks. Let cool and store tightly covered.

CHOC CHIP COOKIES

2 1/4 cups flour
1 teaspoon soda
1 teaspoon salt
1 cup butter, melted
3/4 cup brown sugar
3/4 cup white sugar
1 teaspoon vanilla
2 eggs
1 cup choc chips (or carob chips)
1 cup walnuts (optional)
1 cup oats

Preheat oven to 180°C/350°F. Beat butter and sugar until creamy. Add eggs and vanilla; beat well. Add combined flour, baking soda, and salt; mix well. Stir in choc chips, walnuts, and oats; mix well. Drop dough by rounded tablespoonfuls onto ungreased cookie sheets. Bake 10 to 12 minutes until cookies are almost set. Do not overbake. Cool 1 minute on cookies sheets, then move to wire racks. Let cool and store tightly covered.

FUDGE BROWNIES

1 cup unsalted butter (plus more for pan)
2 cups granulated sugar, packed
4 eggs
2 teaspoons vanilla
3/4 cup flour (plus more for pan)
1 teaspoon vanilla extract
3/4 cup unsweetened cocoa powder (or unsweetened carob powder)
1/2 teaspoon salt
1/2 teaspoon baking powder

Heat oven to 180°C/350°F. Butter and flour baking pan, tapping out excess flour. Melt butter in medium saucepan over medium heat, then remove from heat and stir in sugar followed by eggs and vanilla. Stir in flour, cocoa, baking powder, and salt, adding slowly. Stir until batter is smooth and uniform, about 1 minute. Spread batter into prepared baking pan, smoothing to fill pan evenly. Bake for 35 to 40 minutes, until toothpick or skewer inserted 3/4 inch into corner comes out with few moist clumps. Cool in pan on rack, then cut and serve.

APPLE TEACAKE

2 large apples, chopped
1 cup sugar
1 cup raisins
1 1/2 cups self-raising flour
1 teaspoon mixed spice
2 eggs
2 tablespoons unsalted butter

Preheat oven to 180°C/350°F. Melt butter in medium saucepan and cool. Mix all dry ingredients into bowl and make well in center of mixture. Once butter is cooled, beat eggs lightly and then mix into the dry ingredients. Place mixture in a well-greased baking pan; bake until golden brown and toothpick is clean after inserting in center of cake.

CHOCOLATE CUSTARD PIE

1 pack Marie's or milk biscuits
1/3 cup butter
2 tablespoons sugar
3 tablespoons custard powder
1/3 cup sugar
2 tablespoons cocoa powder (or carob powder)
2 cups milk
Handful chocolate chips or dots (or carob chips)

Crush biscuits into powder; add sugar. Mix in butter and press into pie dish. Mix cocoa, custard powder, and sugar with 1/2 cup milk. Bring remaining milk to a boil. Return to low heat. Add custard powder mixture and stir constantly until thick. Remove from heat. Immediately pour filling into piecrust and refrigerate until fully set. Sprinkle chocolate chips on top.

APPLE PIE

2 cups white flour, plus additional 1/2 cup
1 cup margarine or butter
1/2 cup ice-cold water
1/2 teaspoon salt
8 to 10 apples
1/4 cup margarine or butter
1/2 cup brown sugar
2 or 3 tablespoons flour

In a large mixing bowl, cut flour, salt, and margarine together with fork. Add ice-cold water a little at a time while mixing together. Mix just until dough comes together. Set aside. Peel and cut apples into thin slices. Place in pan on stove with margarine (or butter). Add brown sugar. Simmer apples until soft. Add 1 tablespoon flour at a time until syrup is thick. Roll crust out on floured surface. Place bottom crust in pie pan and add apples. Place top crust. Bake at 180°C/350°F for 30 to 40 minutes or until crust is lightly brown on top.

UPSIDE-DOWN CAKE

2 1/2 tablespoons unsalted butter, plus extra for the tin
1 1/2 cups sugar
2 tablespoons water
2 large mangoes, peeled, and sliced into wedges
3/4 cup unsalted butter, softened
3 eggs, beaten
2 1/2 cups plain flour
2 teaspoons baking powder
Pinch of salt
1/3 cup milk, room temperature

Heat oven to 180°C/350°F. Butter a solid-based round cake tin. Put 1/2 sugar and water in a small saucepan over a low heat to allow the sugar to dissolve. Bring to boil and continue to cook without stirring until the sugar has turned a deep caramel color. Add the 2 1/2 tablespoons of butter and mix. Pour immediately into the cake tin, covering the base with an even layer of caramel. Leave to cool. Arrange the mango slices over the hard caramel in the cake tin. Mix the butter and sugar until pale and fluffy. Gradually add the beaten eggs, mixing well between each addition. Sieve the flour, baking powder, and a pinch of salt together and fold into the cake mixture. Add the milk and mix until smooth. Carefully spoon the cake mixture over the mango slices and level. Bake for about 45 to 50 minutes or until a skewer inserted into the middle of the cake comes out clean. Allow the cake to cool in the tin for 5 minutes before turning out onto a serving dish.

BISCOTTI

1/4 cup butter
1/2 cup white sugar
3 eggs
1 teaspoon vanilla essence
3 cups plain flour
Pinch of salt
1 teaspoon baking powder
1/4 cup almonds/macadamia nuts, chopped

Preheat oven to 165°C/330°F. In a large bowl, cream the butter and sugar together. Add eggs one at a time; beat until fluffy. Stir in the vanilla. Sift together the flour, baking powder, and salt. Add them to the egg mixture along with the chopped almonds/macadamia nuts. Stir with a spoon and, as the dough comes together, knead by hand. Divide the dough into 2 parts. Roll each piece into a log about 10 inches long. Place logs onto baking trays, 2 to a sheet, the long way. Flatten the logs out until they are about 3 inches wide with a slight hump going down the middle. Bake for 25 to 30 minutes in the preheated oven; loaves should be firm. Cut the loaves into diagonal slices 1/2 inch wide, place the slices onto the baking trays, and return to the oven. Toast on one side, then turn them over to do the other side. This will take about 7 to 10 minutes.

INDEX